DAVID ROBERTS

VIEWS OF EGYPT AND NUBIA

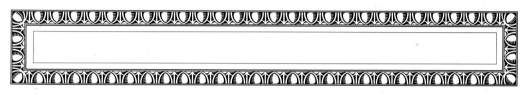

THE HUNTINGTON LIBRARY • A BOOK OF POSTCARDS

POMEGRANATE ARTBOOKS ꜥ•ꜥ SAN FRANCISCO

Pomegranate Artbooks
Box 6099
Rohnert Park, CA 94927

Pomegranate Europe Ltd.
Fullbridge House
Maldon, Essex CM9 7LE
England

ISBN 0-87654-363-8
Pomegranate Catalog No. A784

Pomegranate publishes books of
postcards on a wide range of subjects.
Please write to the publisher for more information.

Designed by Allen Boyce Eddington
Printed in Korea

06 05 04 03 02 01 00 99 98 97   12 11 10 9 8 7 6 5 4 3

The reproductions presented here are the work of Scottish artist David Roberts (1796–1864). They are taken from *Views of Egypt and Nubia*, the final section of his monumental *The Holy Land: Syria, Idumea, Arabia, Egypt and Nubia*. Published in installments between 1842 and 1849, this work contains 250 lithographs developed from sketches Roberts made during an expedition to the Near East in 1838–1839. This series of lithographs represented the most comprehensive assortment of views of the Near East published to that date and is widely considered to be one of the finest examples of the art of tinted lithography.

Prior to his journey to the Near East, Roberts had produced a few largely imaginative paintings utilizing Egyptian architectural elements. But once on site, and pledged to topographical accuracy, he confronted a landscape decidedly unfriendly to the conventions of the picturesque: stark monuments in a sparse and colorless landscape. He employed devices and a certain license to achieve a heightened visual impact. Human figures were employed both to add color and to manipulate scale. He exaggerated the height and width of buildings by altering proportions, moving stones and sometimes even repositioning monuments, as he did with the Sphinx in *Approach of the Simoom, Desert of Gizeh*, and his love for decorative design apparently tempted him at times to supply missing details, as seen in the faces of the figures on the columns in *View from Under the Portico of the Temple of Dendera*.

Roberts's breathtaking lithographs of the Egyptian landscape, interpretative though they may be, nevertheless evoke a strong sense of the ancient monuments he depicts. This book of postcards presents thirty of Roberts's stunning images, all from the collection of The Huntington Library.

Grand View of the Great Temple of Aboosimbel, Nubia.

VIEWS OF EGYPT AND NUBIA

David Roberts (Scottish, 1796–1864)
Front Elevation of the Great Temple of Abu Simbel, Nubia
Color lithograph

Pomegranate, Box 6099, Rohnert Park, CA 94927

Temple of Edfou, ancient Apollinopolis Magna, Egypt.

DAVID ROBERTS R.A.

VIEWS OF EGYPT AND NUBIA

David Roberts (Scottish, 1796–1864)
Temple of Edfou, Ancient Appolinopolis, Upper Egypt
Color lithograph

Pomegranate, Box 6099, Rohnert Park, CA 94927

General View of the Ruins of Luxor, from the Nile.   Thebes, Novr 25th   1838

VIEWS OF EGYPT AND NUBIA

David Roberts (Scottish, 1796–1864)
General View of the Ruins of Luxor, from the Nile
Color lithograph

Pomegranate, Box 6099, Rohnert Park, CA 94927

Grand Approach to the Temple of Philæ, Nubia

VIEWS OF EGYPT AND NUBIA

David Roberts (Scottish, 1796–1864)
Grand Approach to the Temple of Philae, Nubia
Color lithograph

Pomegranate, Box 6099, Rohnert Park, CA 94927

Medinet Abou, Thebes. Dec. 5th 1838.

VIEWS OF EGYPT AND NUBIA

David Roberts (Scottish, 1796–1864)
Medinet Abou, Thebes
Color lithograph

Pomegranate, Box 6099, Rohnert Park, CA 94927

Entrance to the Tombs of the Kings of Thebes, Bab el-Melouk

VIEWS OF EGYPT AND NUBIA

David Roberts (Scottish, 1796–1864)
Entrance to the Tombs of the Kings of Thebes, Biban-el-Molook
Color lithograph

Pomegranate, Box 6099, Rohnert Park, CA 94927

Views of Egypt and Nubia

David Roberts (Scottish, 1796–1864)
Pyramids of Gizeh
Color lithograph

Pomegranate, Box 6099, Rohnert Park, CA 94927

VIEWS OF EGYPT AND NUBIA

David Roberts (Scottish, 1796–1864)
Dayr el Medeeneh, Thebes
Color lithograph

Pomegranate, Box 6099, Rohnert Park, CA 94927

VIEWS OF EGYPT AND NUBIA

David Roberts (Scottish, 1796–1864)
Remains of the Portico of the Temple of Kom Ombo
Color lithograph

Pomegranate, Box 6099, Rohnert Park, CA 94927

VIEWS OF EGYPT AND NUBIA

David Roberts (Scottish, 1796–1864)
View Under the Grand Portico of the Temple of Philae, Nubia
Color lithograph

Pomegranate, Box 6099, Rohnert Park, CA 94927

Views of Egypt and Nubia

David Roberts (Scottish, 1796–1864)
Karnak, Thebes, November 29, 1838
Color lithograph

Pomegranate, Box 6099, Rohnert Park, CA 94927

VIEWS OF EGYPT AND NUBIA

David Roberts (Scottish, 1796–1864)
Karnak, Thebes, November 27, 1838
Color lithograph

Pomegranate, Box 6099, Rohnert Park, CA 94927

VIEWS OF EGYPT AND NUBIA

David Roberts (Scottish, 1796–1864)
View from Under the Portico of the Temple of Dendera
Color lithograph

Pomegranate, Box 6099, Rohnert Park, CA 94927

VIEWS OF EGYPT AND NUBIA

David Roberts (Scottish, 1796–1864)
Approach of the Simoom, Desert of Gizeh
Color lithograph

Pomegranate, Box 6099, Rohnert Park, CA 94927

General View of The Island of Philœ, Nubia. Nov 14th 1838.

VIEWS OF EGYPT AND NUBIA

David Roberts (Scottish, 1796–1864)
General View of the Island of Philae, Nubia
Color lithograph

Pomegranate, Box 6099, Rohnert Park, CA 94927

Interior of the Temple of Aboo Simbel.

VIEWS OF EGYPT AND NUBIA

David Roberts (Scottish, 1796–1864)
Interior of the Temple of Abu Simbel
Color lithograph

Pomegranate, Box 6099, Rohnert Park, CA 94927

View from under the Portico of the Temple of Edfu, Upper Egypt

VIEWS OF EGYPT AND NUBIA

David Roberts (Scottish, 1796–1864)
View from Under the Portico of the Temple of Edfou, Upper Egypt
Color lithograph

Pomegranate, Box 6099, Rohnert Park, CA 94927

VIEWS OF EGYPT AND NUBIA

David Roberts (Scottish, 1796–1864)
Statues of Memnon at Thebes, During the Inundation
Color lithograph

Pomegranate, Box 6099, Rohnert Park, CA 94927

Views of Egypt and Nubia

David Roberts (Scottish, 1796–1864)
The Great Sphinx, Pyramids of Gizeh
Color lithograph

Pomegranate, Box 6099, Rohnert Park, CA 94927

Views of Egypt and Nubia

David Roberts (Scottish, 1796–1864)
The Hypaethral Temple at Philae, Called the Bed of Pharaoh
Color lithograph

Pomegranate, Box 6099, Rohnert Park, CA 94927

VIEWS OF EGYPT AND NUBIA

David Roberts (Scottish, 1796–1864)
Temple at Esneh
Color lithograph

Pomegranate, Box 6099, Rohnert Park, CA 94927

The Great Temple of Aboosimbel, Nubia

VIEWS OF EGYPT AND NUBIA

David Roberts (Scottish, 1796–1864)
The Great Temple of Abu Simbel, Nubia
Color lithograph

Pomegranate, Box 6099, Rohnert Park, CA 94927

VIEWS OF EGYPT AND NUBIA

David Roberts (Scottish, 1796–1864)
Temple of Dendera
Color lithograph

Pomegranate, Box 6099, Rohnert Park, CA 94927

VIEWS OF EGYPT AND NUBIA

David Roberts (Scottish, 1796–1864)
Grand Portico of the Temple of Philae, Nubia
Color lithograph

Pomegranate, Box 6099, Rohnert Park, CA 94927